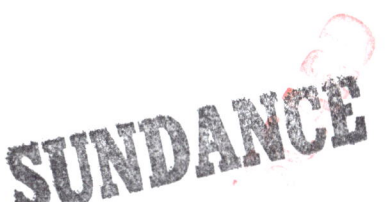

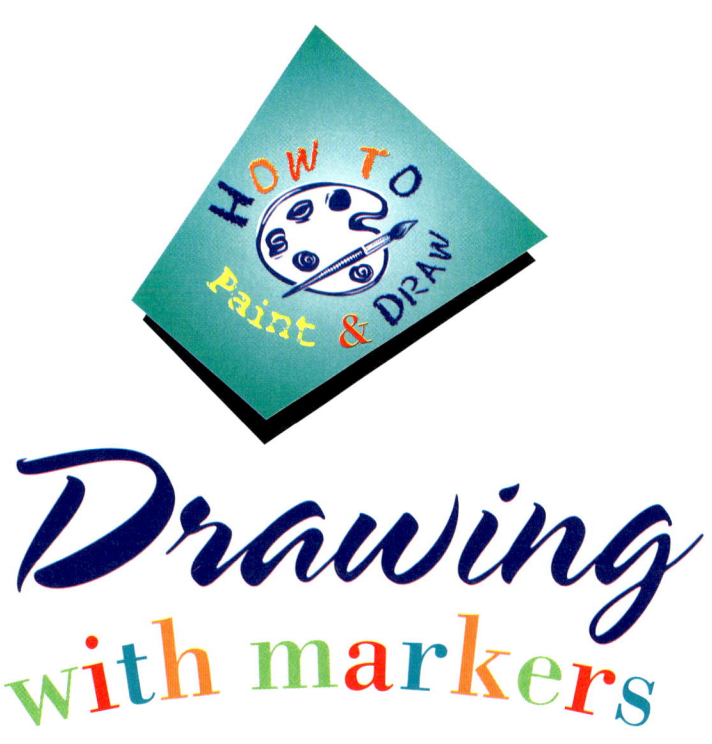

Drawing with markers

Paige Henson

The Rourke Press, Inc.
Vero Beach, Florida 32964

© 1999 The Rourke Press, Inc.

All rights reserved. No part of this book may be reproduced or utilized in any form or by any means, electronic or mechanical including photocopying, recording, or by any information storage and retrieval system without permission in writing from the publisher.

ART CREDITS:
Bob Hochgertel, Kingfish Studios: pages 5, 10, 12, 13, 14
Charlie Beyl, Kingfish Studios: 4, 9, 11, 19, 22, 23, 24, 25, 26
Joseph Pinaud: 9, 15, 16, 17, 19, 21, 27
Jim Royal, D.C. Comics: page 20

PHOTOGRAPHY:
Glen Benson and East Coast Studios

PRODUCED & DESIGNED BY:
East Coast Studios, Merritt Island, Florida

EDITORIAL SERVICES:
Susan Albury

ACKNOWLEDGEMENTS:
East Coast Studios would like to thank Gardendale Elementary School, Merritt Island, for their assistance in this project.

Library of Congress Cataloging-in-Publication Data

Henson, Paige, 1949-
   Drawing with markers / by Paige Henson
     p. cm. — (How to paint and draw)
   Includes bibliographical references and index.
   Summary: Provides techniques and advice on drawing with marking pens, and suggests several projects to try.
   ISBN 1-57103-309-2
   1. Dry marker drawing—Technique Juvenile literature. 2. Felt marker drawing—Technique Juvenile literature. [1. Felt marker drawing—Technique. 2. Drawing—Technique.] I. Title. II. Series: Henson, Paige, 1949- How to paint and draw.
NC878.H46 1999
741.2'6—dc21   99-30650
                                                                           CIP

Printed in the USA

Contents

CHAPTER 1 Art Tells Stories About Life 4

CHAPTER 2 What Markers to Use 6

CHAPTER 3 Color and Techniques 8

CHAPTER 4 Cartooning Fun 15

CHAPTER 5 Lettering 23

CHAPTER 6 Cleanup 28

Glossary 30

Index & Further Reading 32

Chapter 1
Art Tells Stories About Life

Men and women have told stories and expressed themselves with simple line drawings since the beginning of recorded time. In Europe in the late 1700s, artists first began using drawings to criticize various things they felt were wrong in society and government. Some pictures poked fun of pompous kings and queens and others in high offices. These first political **cartoons** (kahr TOONZ) were circulated in materials printed for the public and were very popular. People loved them!

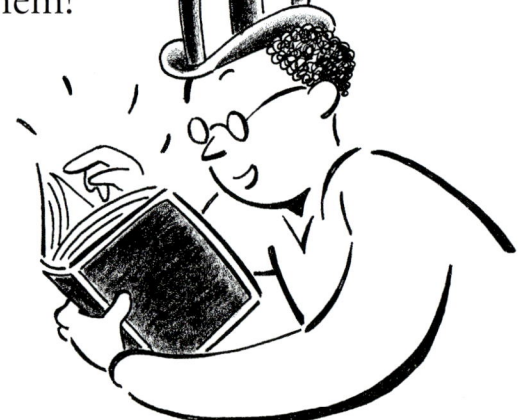

When art markers became popular in this century, illustrators had a fresh, new way to express themselves on paper. Today's **graphic artists** (GRA fik AR tists) often use art markers to sketch out ideas for presentations. In fact, markers and computer software programs are the most frequently used art tools in the modern business world.

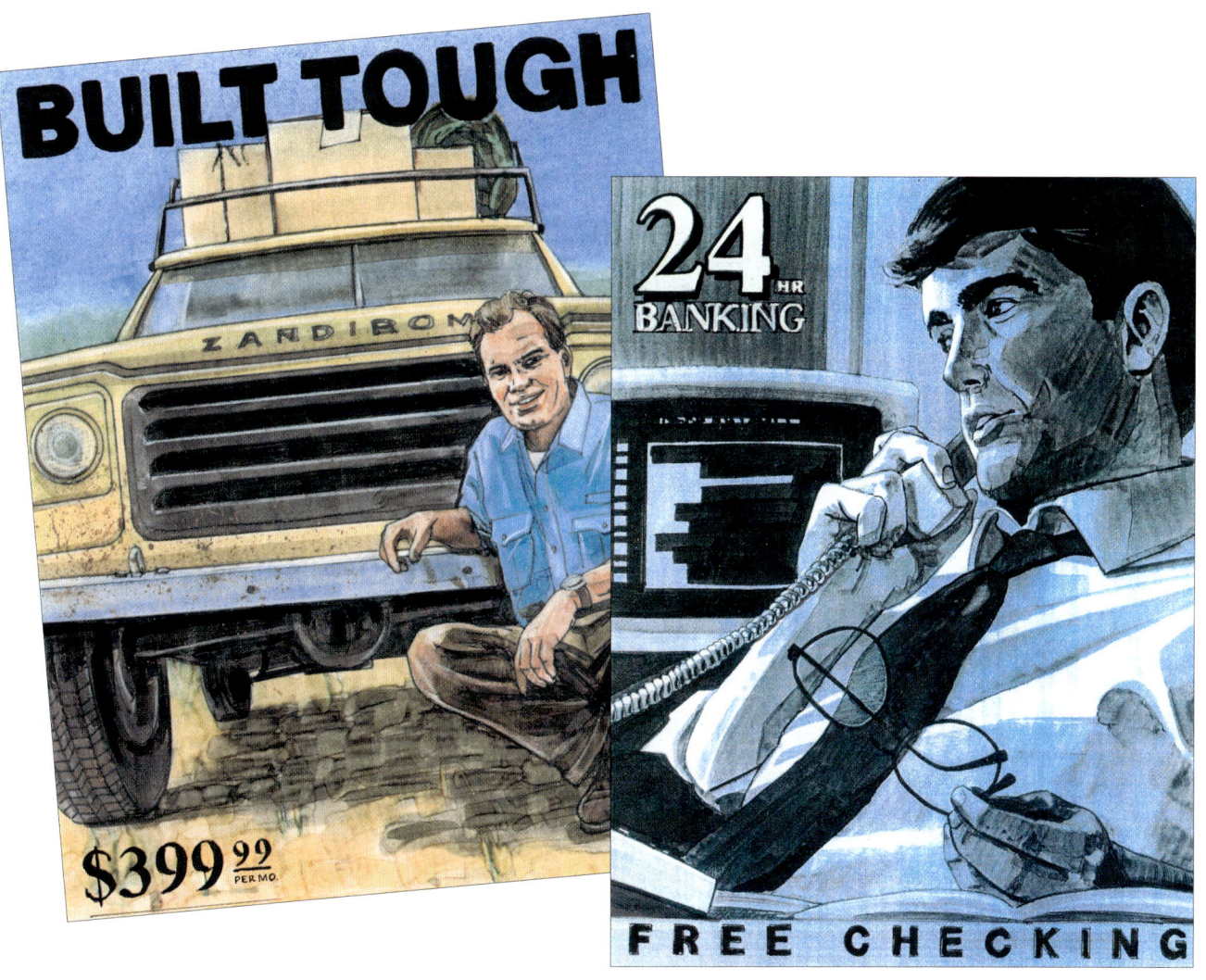

Chapter 2
What Markers to Use

Art markers are popular drawing tools because of their vivid colors, the crisp lines they make, and the many ways in which they can be used. Most graphic artists, fashion designers, book illustrators, architects, and other artistic professionals use art markers at one time or another in their work.

Markers are sold in sets of many sizes and colors. The ink of some can be blended or are available in colors that change when drawn over an original line. For beginners who prefer to draw on paper, the best markers are water-based, meaning the ink can be washed off skin and out of clothes easily, and the colors will not easily bleed through paper. On the other hand, **permanent ink** (PER muh nuhnt INGK) ink markers are ideal for drawing on ceramic tiles, plastic, vinyl, metal, glass, and other surfaces.

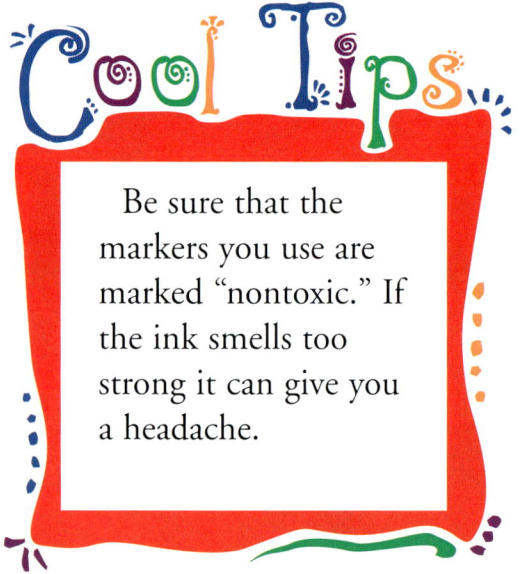

Cool Tips

Be sure that the markers you use are marked "nontoxic." If the ink smells too strong it can give you a headache.

It's best to have both thin and thick pointed markers handy for art projects. Thin-line markers are just right for drawing, writing, and outlining, while broad-line markers are good for coloring in larger areas. Some markers even come in chisel, bullet-shaped, or other special tips for different kinds of projects. As far as colors go, choose the ones you like best—primaries, tropicals, fluorescents, or even shimmery metallics. If you're planning to draw and paint outdoor scenes, you might need extra brown, light blue, and green markers for sky, grass, trees, and bushes.

Choose paper with a flat finish that "holds" color and will not smear the marker ink like a slick, glossy paper might. Paper used for a copy machine or a plain paper fax will do nicely...but be sure to ask permission to use it first! If your markers tend to **bleed** (BLEED) through to the other side of the paper, be sure to put a piece of cardboard underneath.

Chapter 3
Color and Techniques

Sometimes you will want to create pictures that have a realistic look, like some art created with paints, pens, and pencils. Remember, you can blend the ink colors of some types of markers just as you would blend paint.

There are three basic or primary colors from which all other colors begin: red, yellow, and blue.

The three secondary colors, orange, green, and purple, are created by mixing equal amounts of the two primary colors next to it on the color wheel on either side, like this:

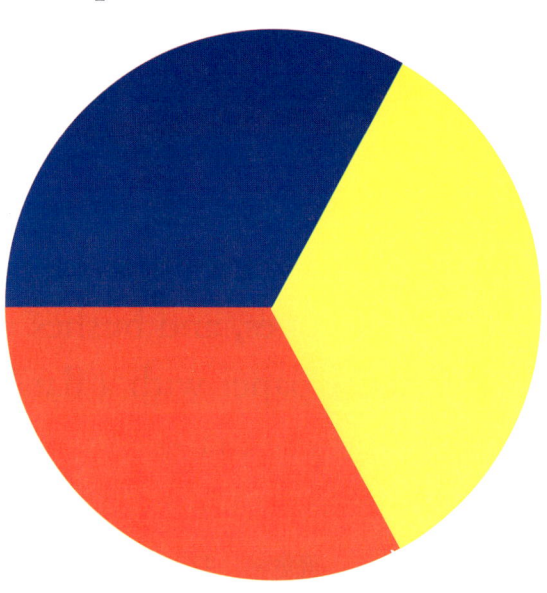

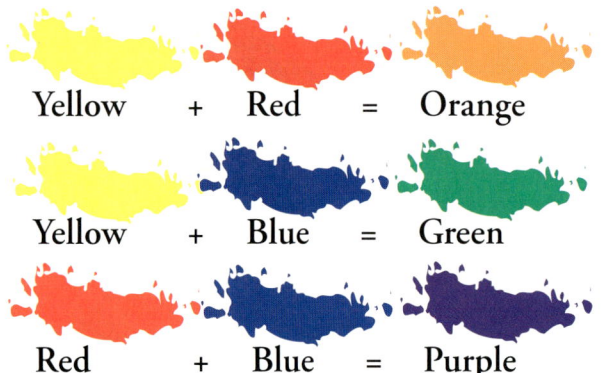

Yellow + Red = Orange

Yellow + Blue = Green

Red + Blue = Purple

Using an art marker with a broad point, you can lay down one color over another to create a new, more intense color.

Because felt-tip pens are almost see-through, this works in much the same way as combining watercolor paint colors. For best results, always lay the lighter color down first, and then overlay it with the darker.

For the top apple, the artist used only one red pen and one brown pen. Notice the different shades of red that can be created by layering and overlapping color from the same pen.

Three to four colors were used in the bottom apple, creating a more realistic look.

Pointillism

You can create variations in color by using this popular artistic technique: **Pointillism** (PWAN tuhl iz uhm) involves putting tiny points of color down side-by-side and very close together so that the viewer's eye mixes the colors to create new ones.

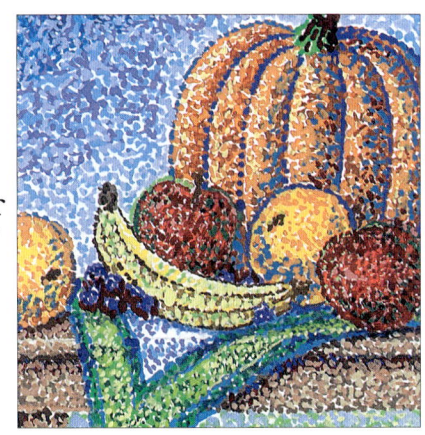

Laying Down Large Areas of Color

Use the back-and-forth, side-to-side method to lay down the lighter color you will be using first. Beginning at the top of the area you are coloring, overlay a second layer using a darker shade of the same color. Stop before you reach the bottom, letting the lighter color beneath show through. Do this again, using an even darker shade, but stop above where the second layer stops. Proceed with this method until you can see a smooth **graduation** (grad juh WAY shun) of color value, from dark to light.

Leaving Some Areas White

The white paper you use can itself become an important part of your art. Remember, you will not be able to create white with your art markers, so leaving some areas uncolored can serve as the white in your picture.

Shading

Shading and shadowing give the objects in your picture **dimension** (duh MEN shun). Without it, things would simply look flat on the page. Observe how **shades** (SHAYDZ) (on the object) are created and **shadows** (SHA dohz) (off the object) are cast when light from a single source—a lamp, the sun, the moon, a flashlight, etc.—falls on the object. Keep in mind that a shadow will always appear on the opposite side of the light source. To build shading, start with the lightest color and add the darker color while the marker ink is still wet. You will use the same overlapping techniques described on page 9.

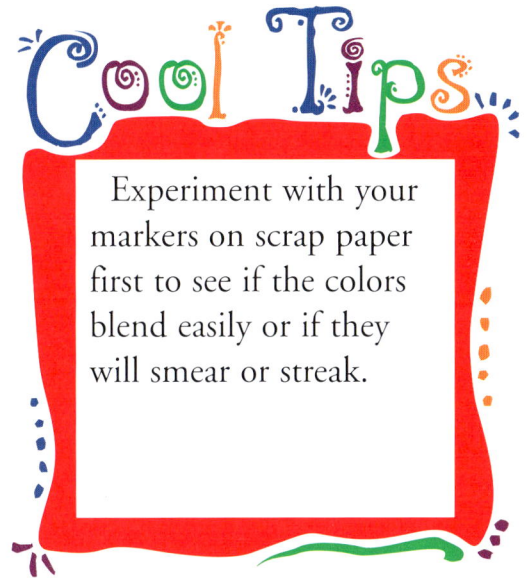

Cool Tips

Experiment with your markers on scrap paper first to see if the colors blend easily or if they will smear or streak.

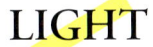
LIGHT

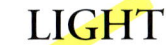
LIGHT

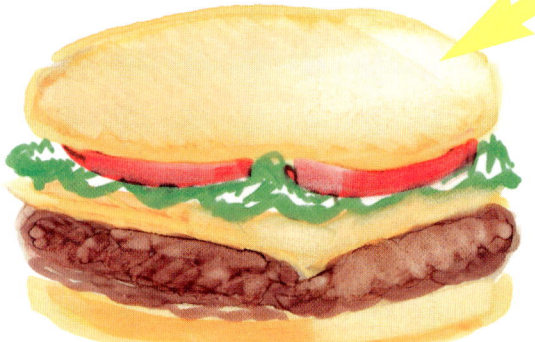

Start with the light colors first. No detail yet.

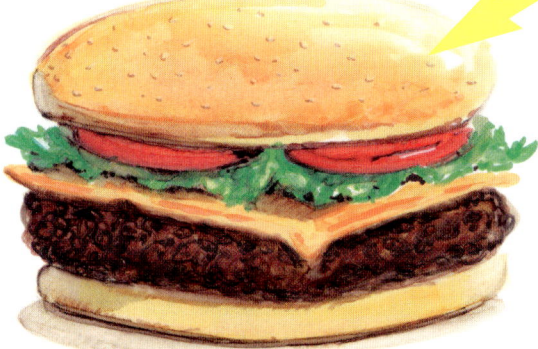

Multiple passes with a marker create deeper colors, shadows, and detail.

Try Drawing a Shiny Car

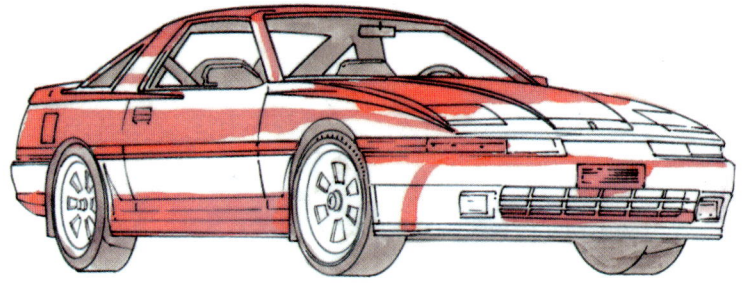

STEP 1 Use a fine tip black marker to draw the car. Elipse templates and french curves will help keep your lines accurate and clean. Making sure the lines are dry, color over them with your base color, using a fairly broad tip pen. Make sure to leave white areas for highlights and reflections.

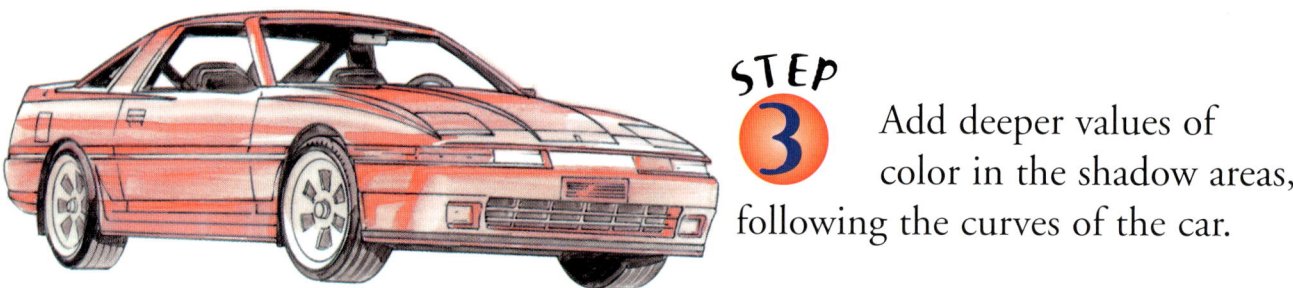

STEP 3 Add deeper values of color in the shadow areas, following the curves of the car.

STEP 3 Now for the details. Add the darkest colors, including black in the tires and trim. Add blue to the windshield, and blue and gray to the chrome wheels. White paint or white pencil can be used for final highlights.

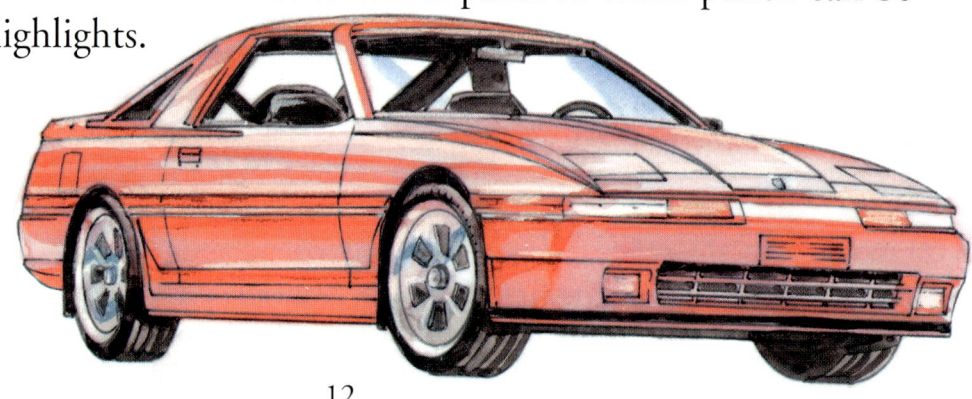

Try Drawing Faces

STEP 1 Start with a basic line drawing, drawn with a fine tip, water-based art marker.

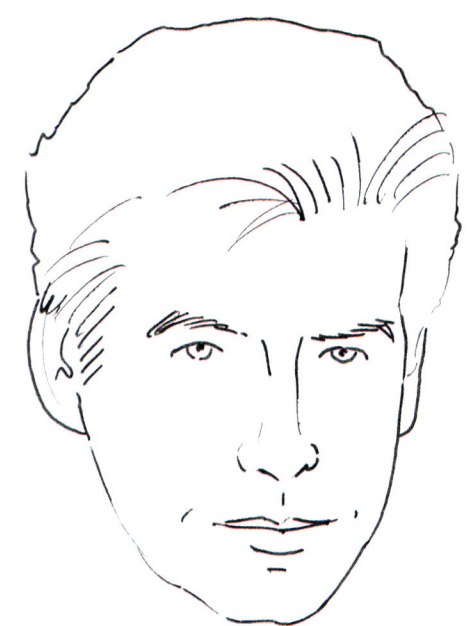

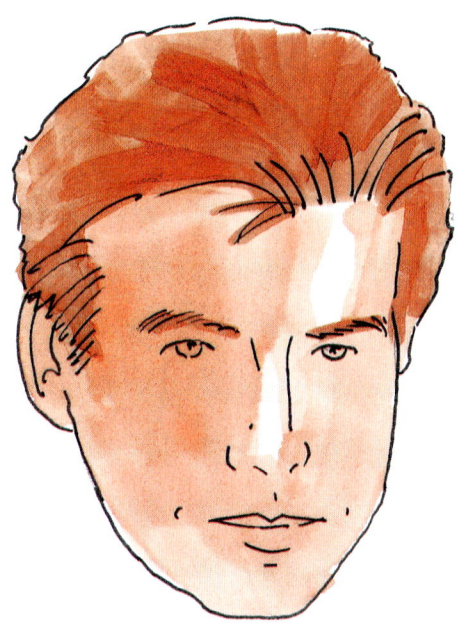

STEP 2 Block in your base colors, allowing the white paper to show through in order to highlight specific areas.

STEP 3 Use darker colors for the shadow areas. You can add texture and highlights with a white colored pencil or white paint.

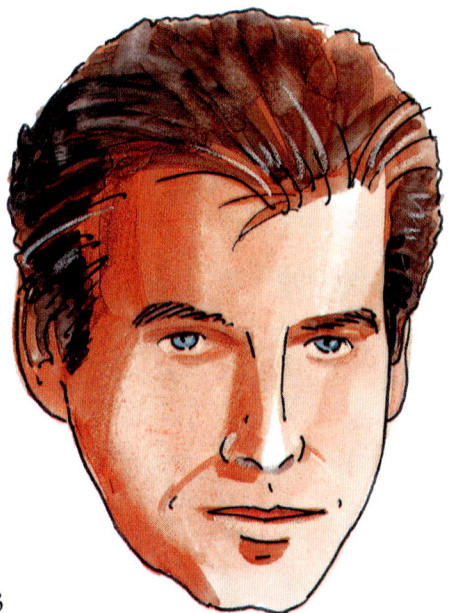

Try Drawing a Sunset

STEP 1 Lay down stripes of the colors you want to use; blue, purple, red, orange, and yellow.

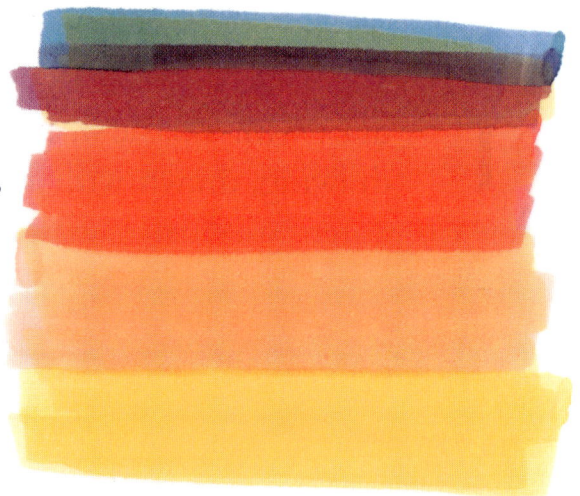

STEP 2 Using a **blender** (BLEN dur), begin blending from the *bottom up!* Carefully overlap each stroke as you work the blend up the page.

STEP 3 Use browns and purples to draw in the clouds. Then, using white paint or a white colored pencil, draw in the sun and the highlights on the clouds.

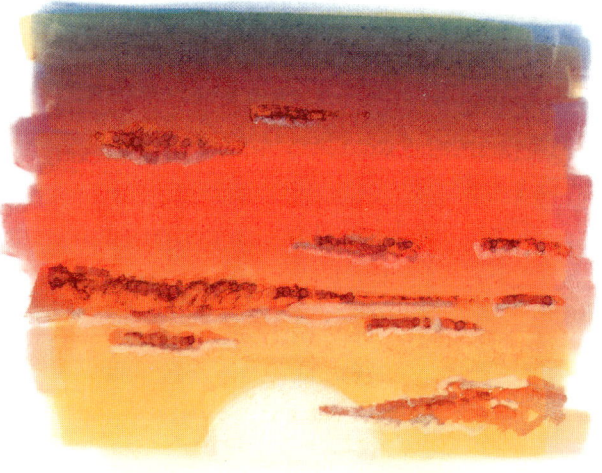

Chapter 4
Cartooning Fun

As we discussed, people often use art to tell stories. Series stories in comic strips or comic books are often drawn by artists using art markers. The stories are drawn in single boxes or frames, and these frames are joined together in panels that show the action of the story unfolding. Of course, "comic" books are not always funny—some are very scary and realistic.

PROJECT

Think of the common characteristics of the characters you draw and use them to your advantage. For instance, what do you first picture in your mind when you think of a caveman? Does he wear a bearskin suit fastened at one shoulder and carry a club?

Or a baby. Does she have a single curl at the top of her head tied with a pink ribbon, and one tiny tooth prominent in front?

These are examples of stereotypes, and cartoonists use them quite a bit!

If cartoon dogs or other animals are the main characters in a strip, they often wear clothes and walk on two legs like humans. If they are not the main character, they usually stand on all fours wagging their tails, panting, and generally looking stupid.

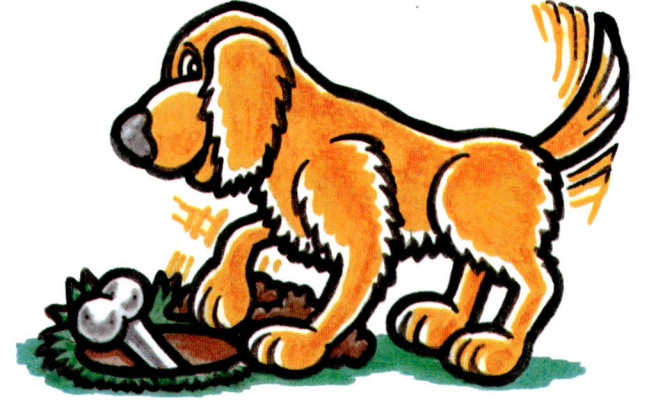

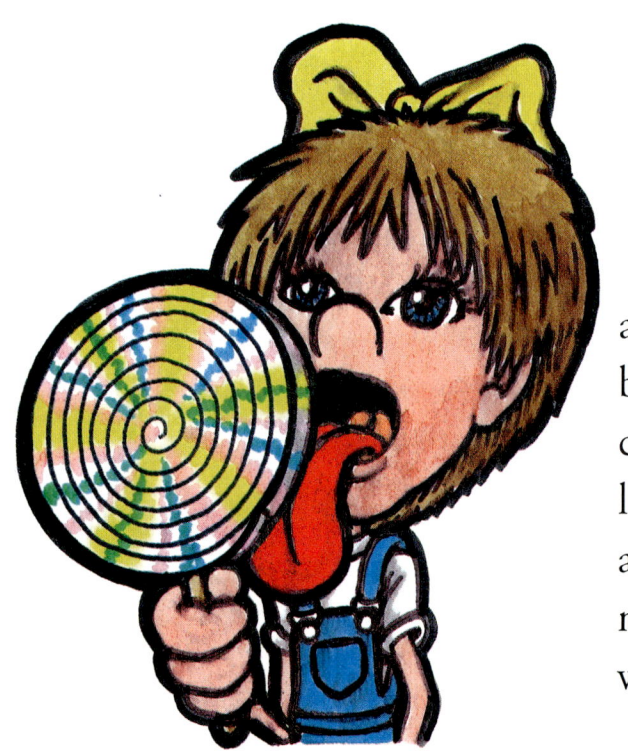

In humorous cartoons, kids' heads are bigger in porportion to their bodies. Study some of your favorite comic books and see how many things like feet, hands facial features, props, and other objects are exaggerated, or made larger and bolder than they would be in real life.

Experiment and Doodle

Experiment with different body shapes, hairdos, and facial expressions by **doodling** (DOOD ling). Doodling is a superfast method of drawing that people do without thinking too much about how things should look. Just let your doodle drawings flow...

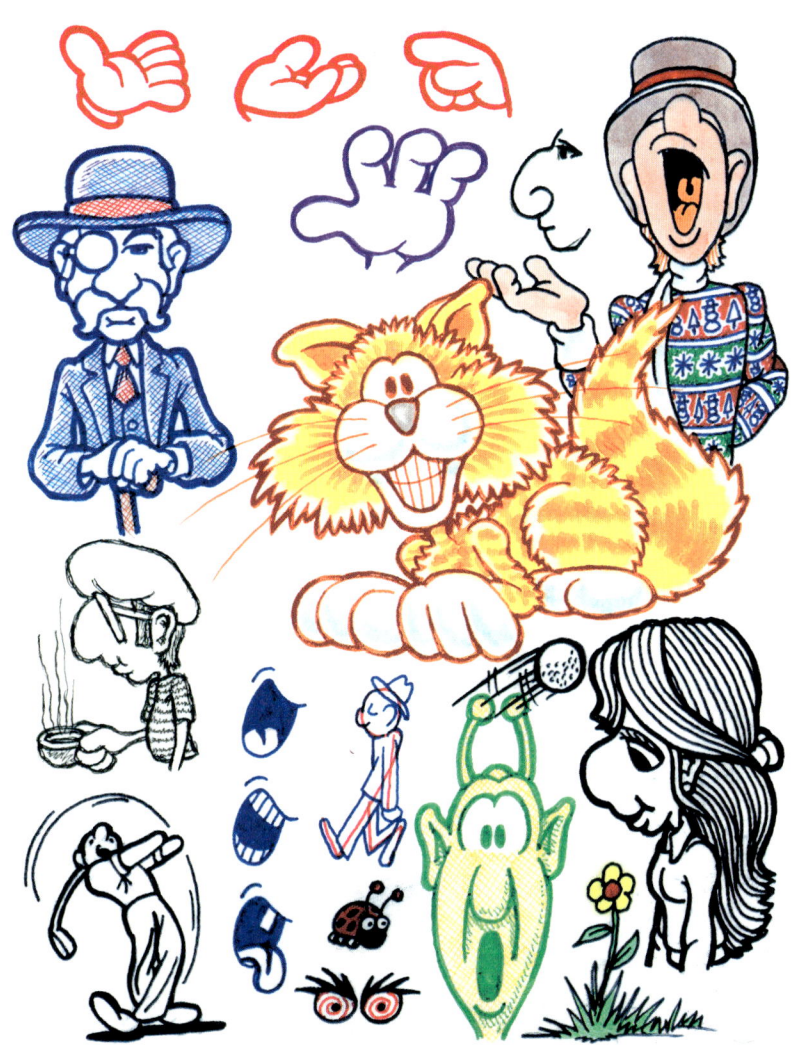

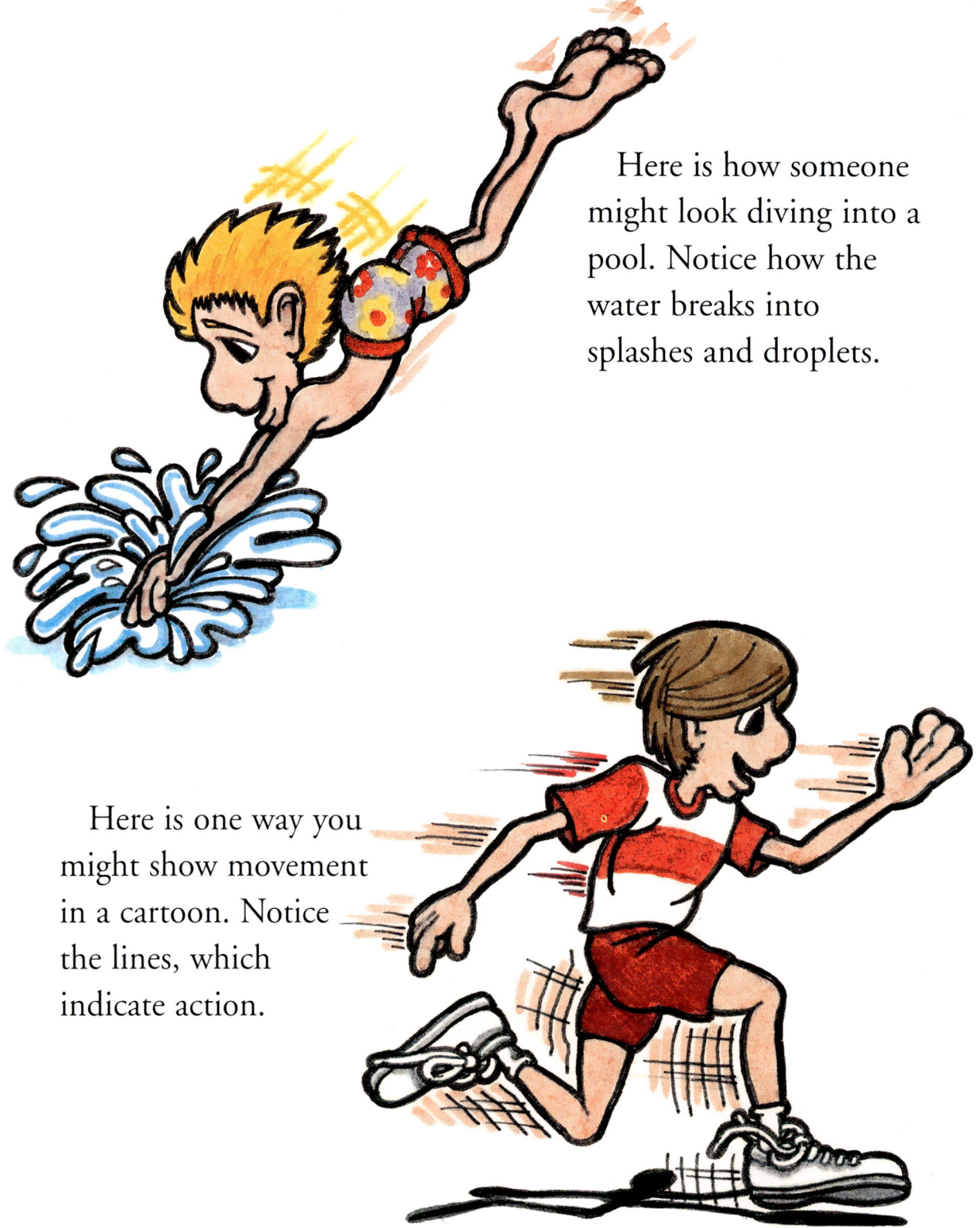

Here is how someone might look diving into a pool. Notice how the water breaks into splashes and droplets.

Here is one way you might show movement in a cartoon. Notice the lines, which indicate action.

Of course, you can also *tell* the reader about the action:

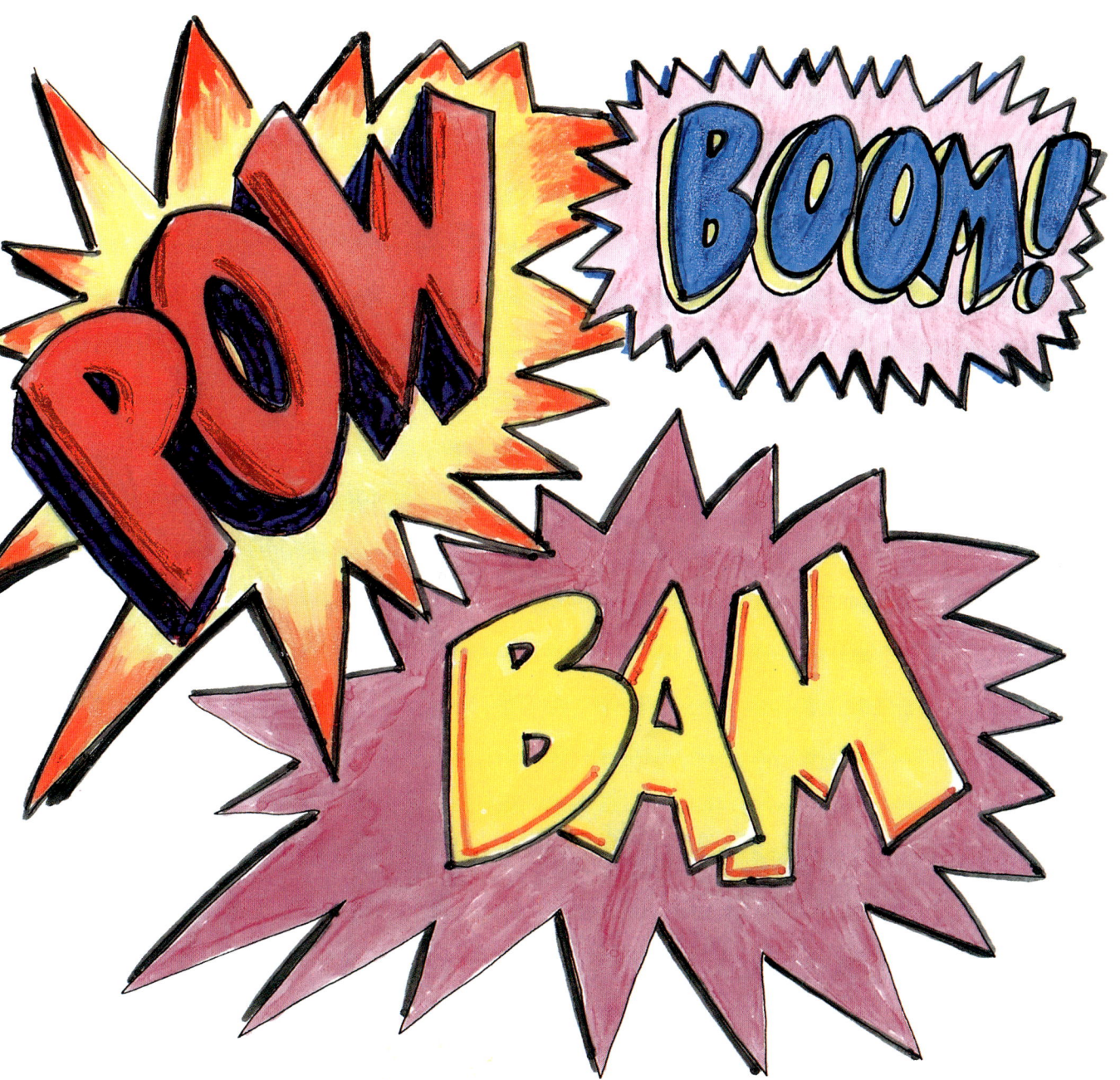

Think of ways to illustrate other sounds.

Comic books are created in several stages. Sometimes one artist draws the graphics, and another adds color.

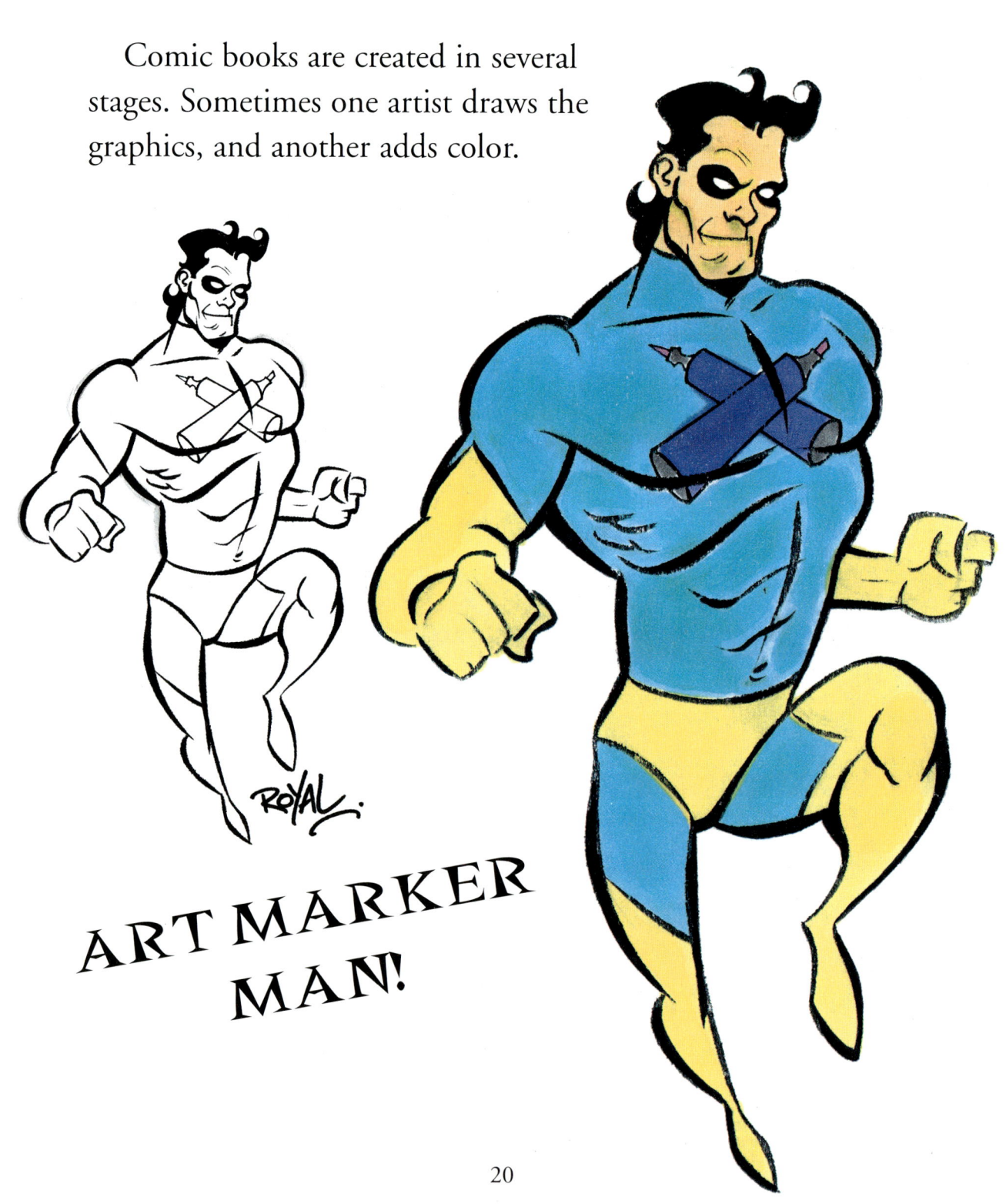

ART MARKER MAN!

Tips for Drawing Your Own Cartoon Story

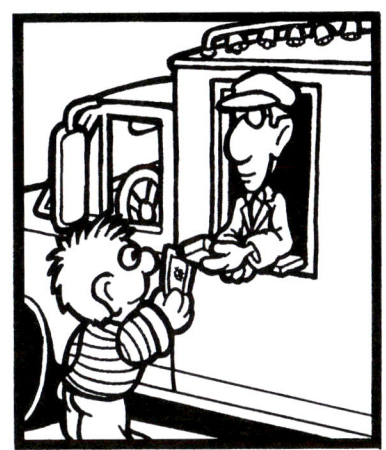 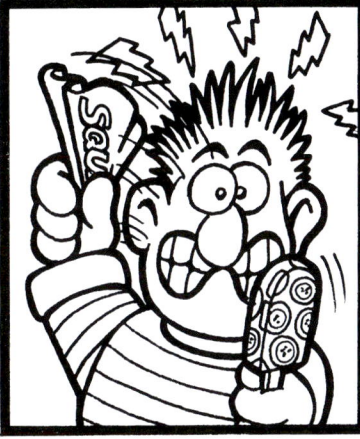 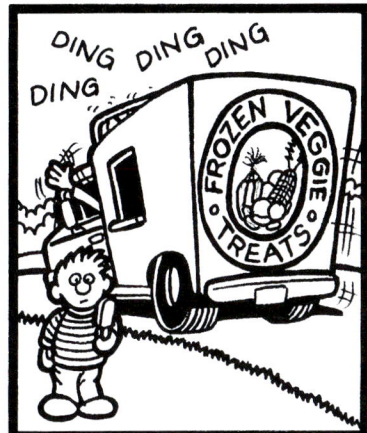

- Begin with a character or two and a short plot or gag to use for your cartoon.
- Using a straightedge, draw all the square or rectangular frames you will need to tell your story.
- Think of a character and how his personality might make him look and act. Keep in mind that your character or characters will have the same body and facial features in every frame.
- Decide on a simple background you'll use in every frame, such as a fence, a yard, a street, or a road—but don't make backgrounds too busy. The main focus should be on your character and what he or she does—or doesn't—do.
- Add cartoon **speech bubbles** (SPEECH BUH buhlz) when people talk; if you need them, add storytelling notes (Later.../Meanwhile..., etc.) at the top or bottom of the frame it applies to.

Create Your Own Space Alien

Do all aliens from outer space look like little green men or Steven Spielberg's ET? We think not! Create a space alien that you can relate to. One that could become famous someday as the main character in your own comic strip! You choose the colors. You choose the features. Name your alien, draw him in several positions. Get to know him well!

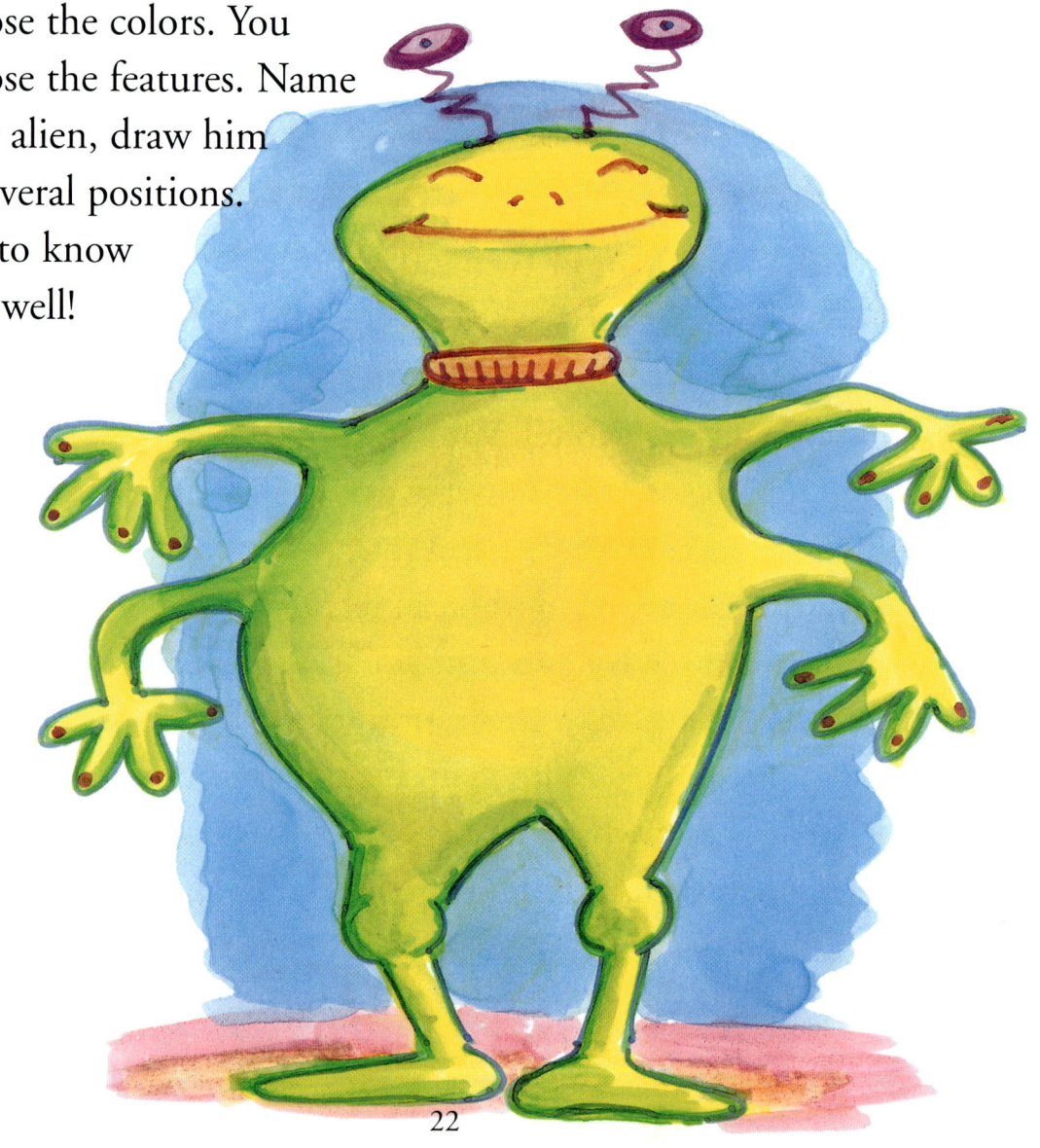

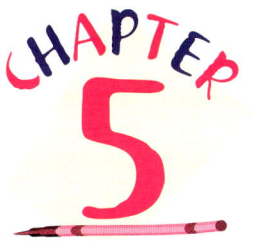

Chapter 5

Lettering

Cool-looking **lettering** (LEH tur ing) is easy to do using art markers.

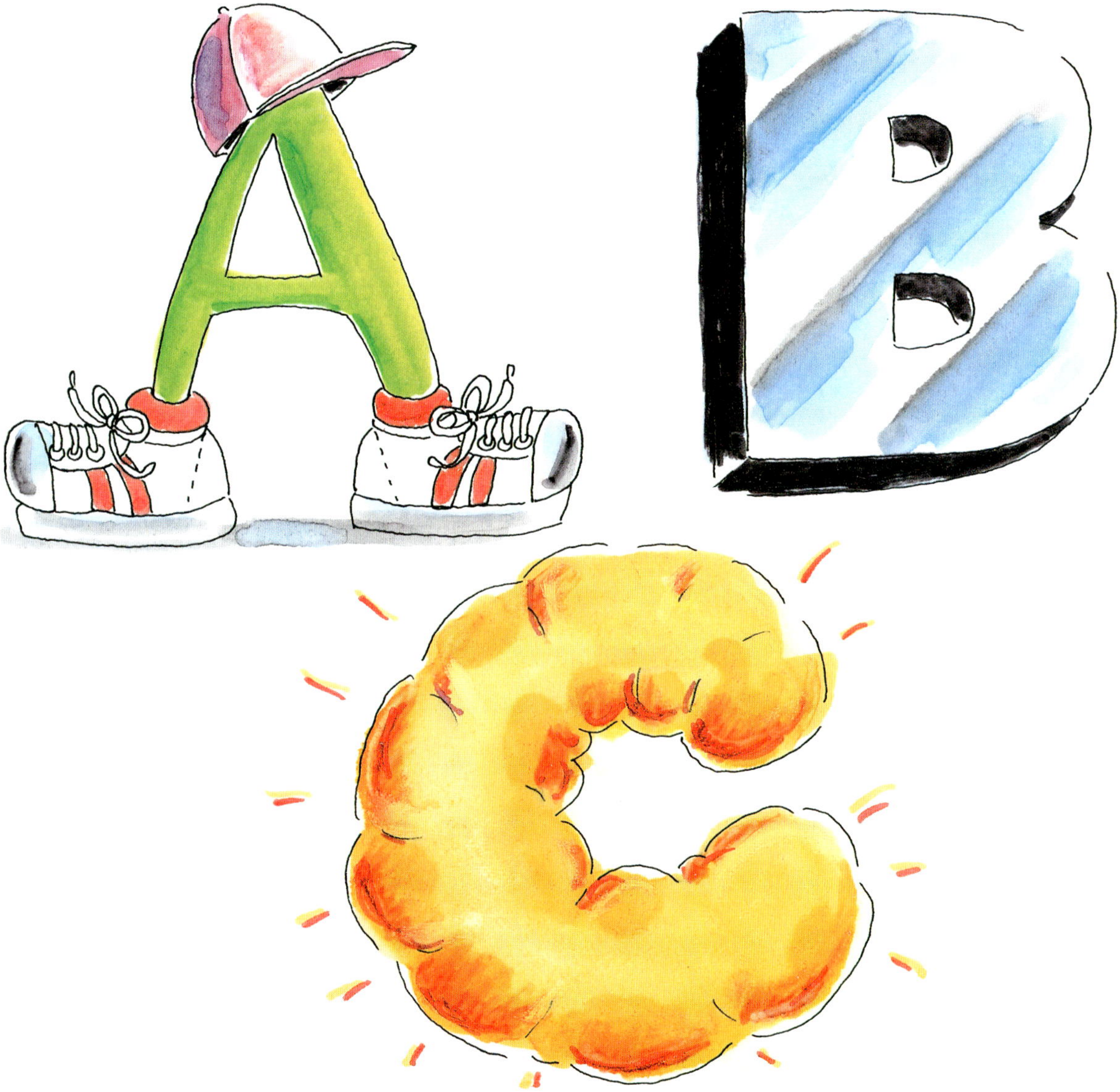

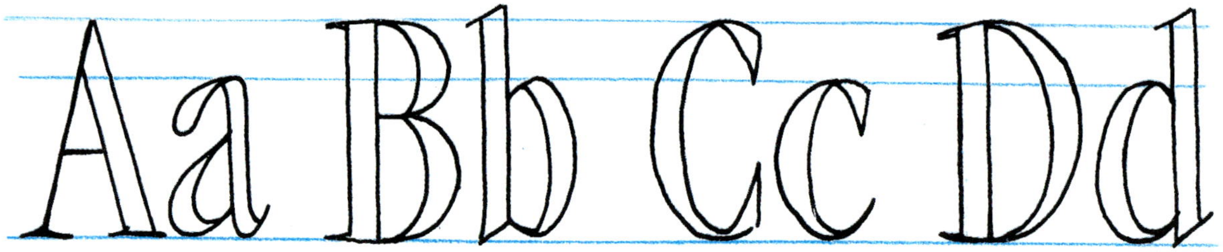

Aa Bb Cc Dd

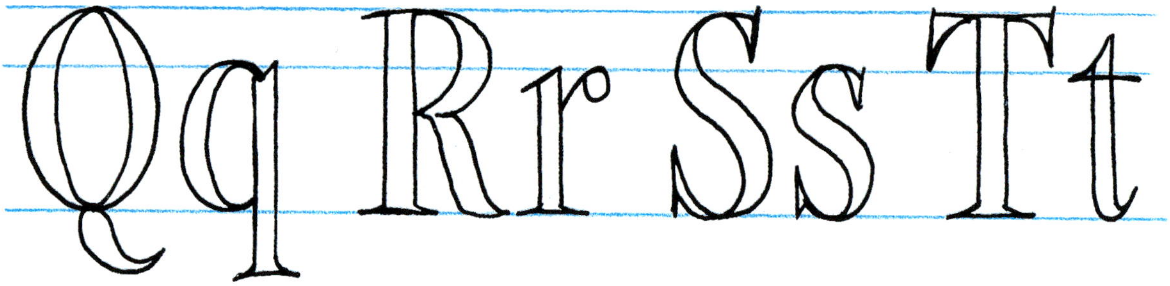

Qq Rr Ss Tt

    Here's how to letter the alphabet, using the basic double-stroke method. To do this, draw two strokes running parallel (side-by-side) to make the thick part of each letter; use single lines to fill in or connect other parts of the letter. If you practice until lettering is easy for you to do, you will be lettering all over the place!

    Using a straightedge lightly draw three horizontal lines (see above) to use as a guide. Use the top and bottom lines as a guide to draw the uppercase (capital) letters, and use the middle and bottom lines as a guide to draw the lowercase letters.

Now, try these letters in 3-D:

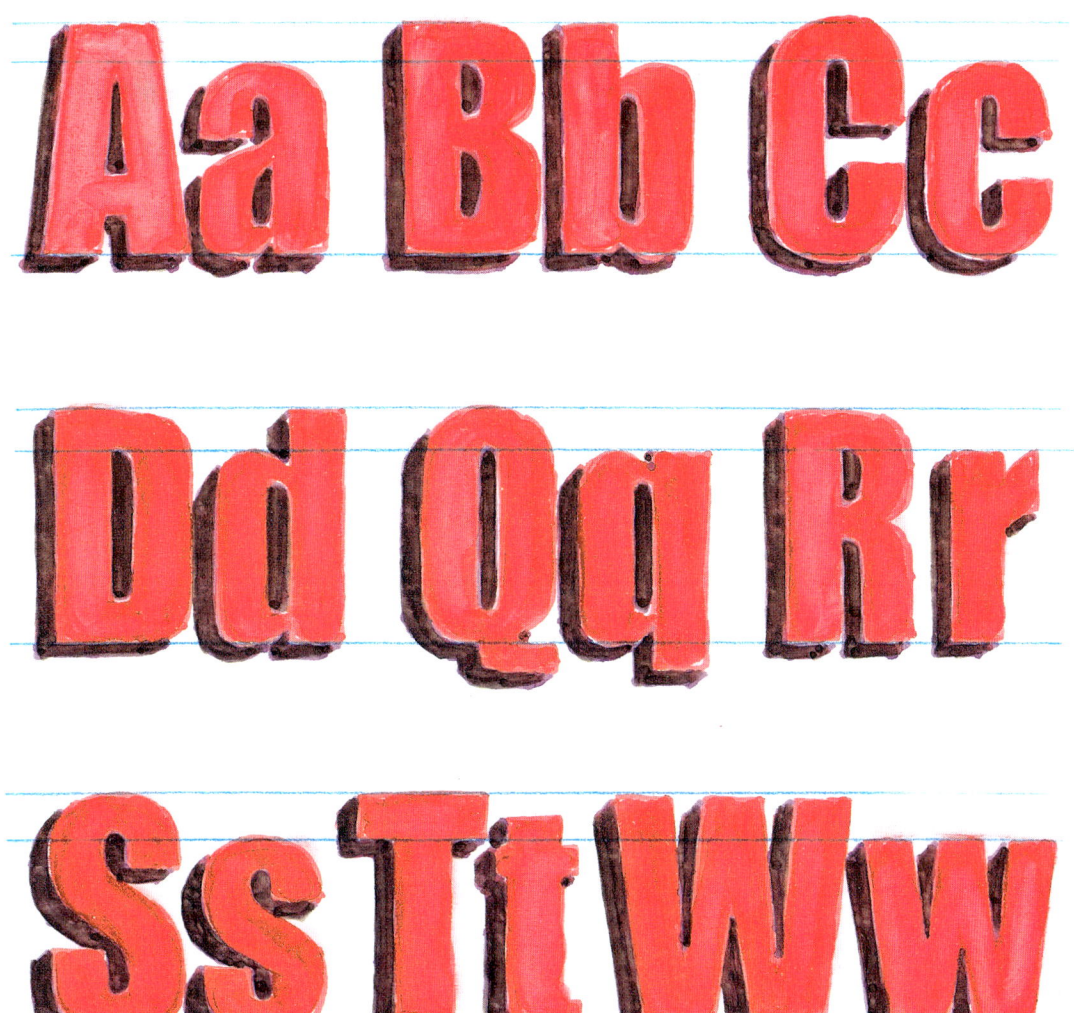

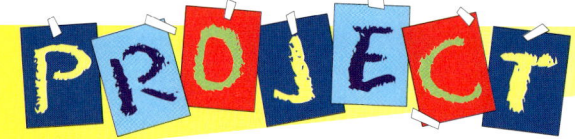

PROJECT

Pretend you are a graphic artist at a big food company. Think of a fun name for a new brand of cookies and, using art markers, design the packaging for the product. The lettering techniques you've practiced should look nice on your new cookie box!

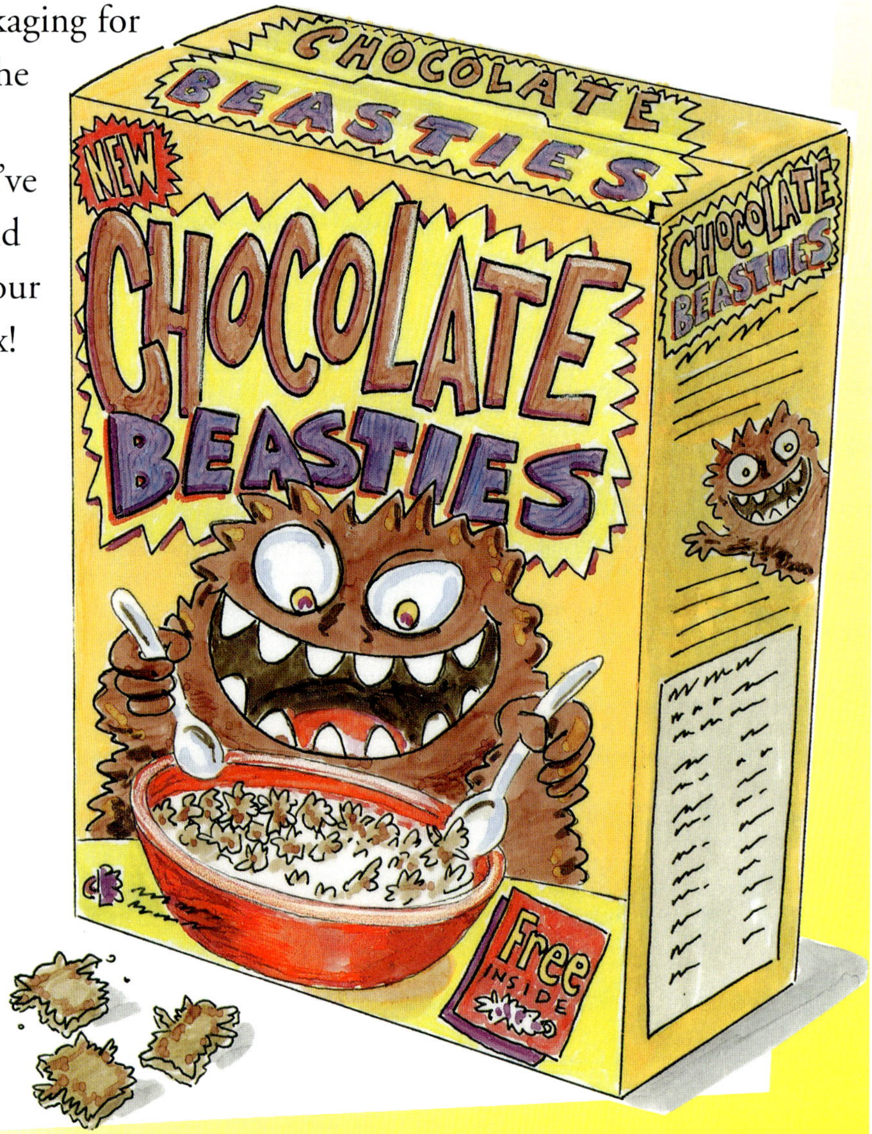

Art with Designs and Emblems

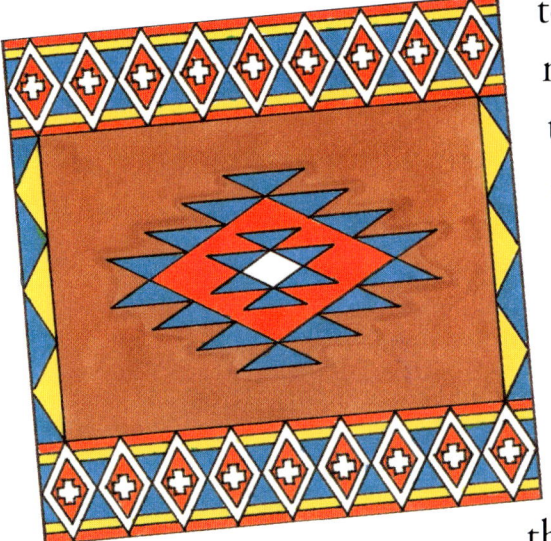

Since the beginning of time, people have decorated their tents, jewelry, clothing, rugs, wall murals, quilts, pottery and even tombstones with artistic patterns and designs. Many of these decorations have magical meanings behind them and represent special objects such as flowers, hearts, leaves, animals, the sun and moon, and other things. You can use art markers to create brilliantly colored designs and emblems of all kinds—from geometric shapes to patterns of great detail.

Using your ruler or straightedge, draw a square using a black, thin-tipped marker. Inside the square, design a pattern that might be used for an early Native-American blanket or a pioneer quilt square.

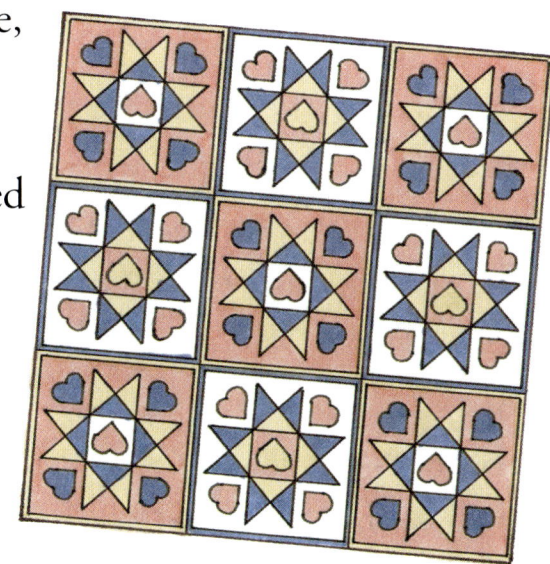

Cleanup

If you have used water-based markers, clean up is just a matter of washing with soap and water. Removing permanent ink from your skin, however, will take more than one or two washings. The most important things to remember are:

1 Recap a marker each time you have finished using it so it will not dry out. When you uncap a marker, keep the top upright and close by so you can find it easily after you have finished with that particular color.

2 Like professional artists do, always store your markers together. Something as simple as a plastic cup works very well—it's inexpensive and the markers can't roll off your desk or shelf.

3 Store any art you want to save in a clean, uncluttered place.

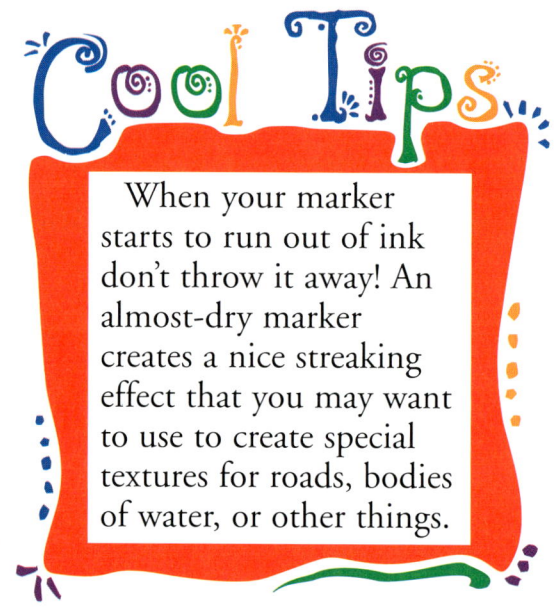

Cool Tips

When your marker starts to run out of ink don't throw it away! An almost-dry marker creates a nice streaking effect that you may want to use to create special textures for roads, bodies of water, or other things.

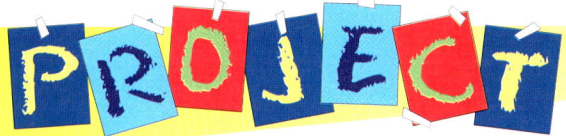

Tile Art

Have an adult ask for leftover or sample ceramic tiles at a home center store. With permanent markers, decorate the tiles using vivid colors. The ink will dry right away, so plan out your art on a sheet of paper beforehand. The completed tiles make colorful hot pads which can be used to protect tabletops from hot food bowls and dishes.

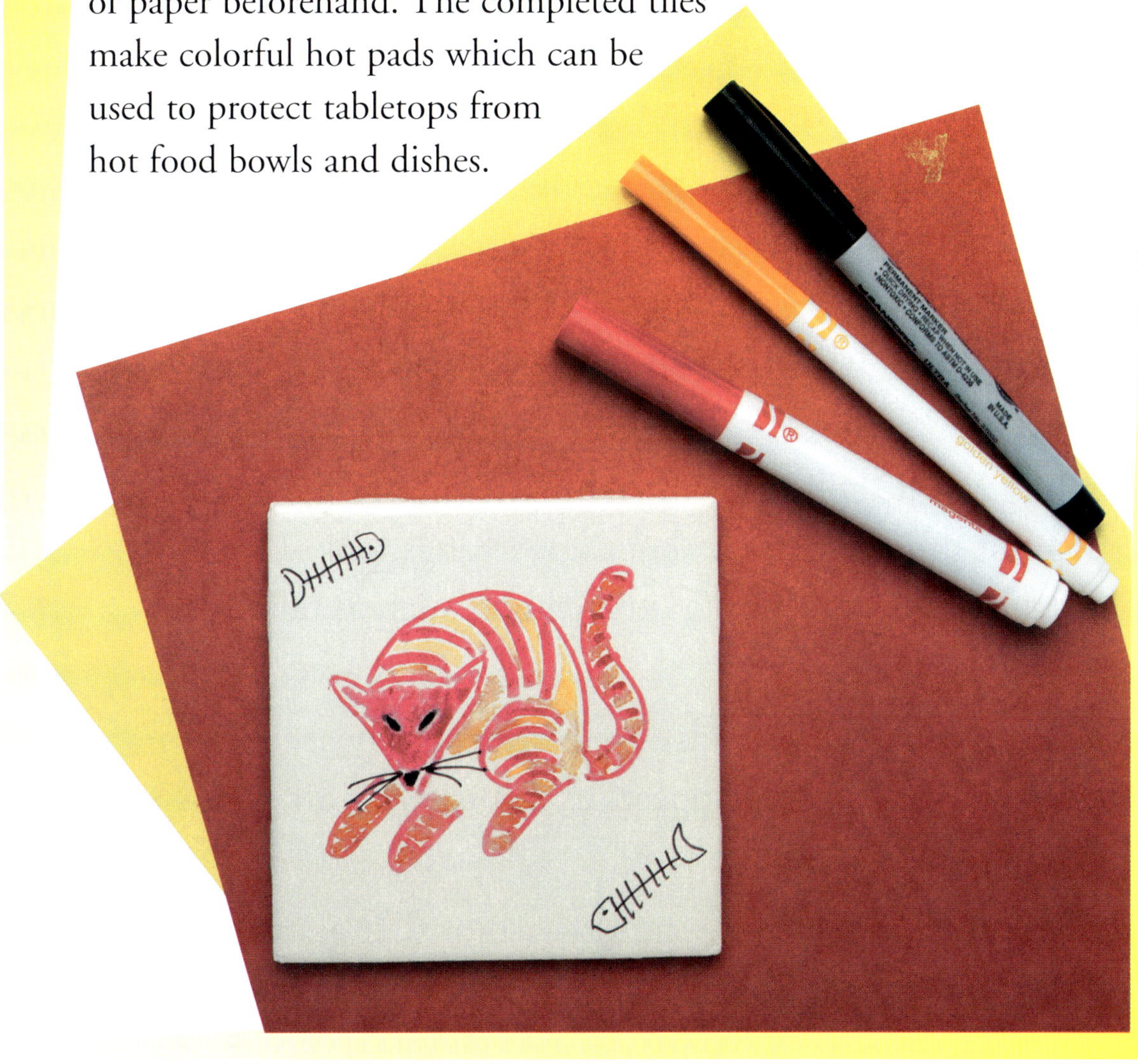

Glossary

bleed (BLEED) — color that shows through on the side of the paper on which you have not drawn. Turn your paper over to see if you have a "bleed" of color.

blender (BLEN dur) — a marker containing clear, colorless "ink" used for blending and softening colors in a marker drawing

cartoon (kahr TOON) — originally a plan for a picture to be painted; today it refers to a single line drawing or series of drawings that tell a story or give a message. Many—but not all—cartoons are humorous.

doodling (DOOD ling) — sketching small, simple graphics without thinking much about how things look. People often doodle while doing other things such as talking on the phone.

dimension (duh MEN shun) — in art, the way an object in a drawing or painting appears as if it extends off the paper instead of looking flat

graduation (grad juh WAY shun) — color that gradually fades into another color

graphic artist (GRA fik AR tist) — one who uses tools such as art markers, pen and ink, a camera, or computer software to create graphics

lettering (LEH tur ing) — drawing the letters of the alphabet in an artistic or interesting way

permanent ink (PUR muh nuhnt INGK) — ink that is permanent and cannot easily be washed off skin or fabric

pointillism (PWAN tuhl iz uhm) — a style of painting that places "points" or dots of two or three colors very close together to create yet another color in the eye of the viewer

shade (SHAYD) — the darker area of an object in a drawing or painting; usually the part farthest from a source of light shining on the object

shadow (SHA doh) — a dark area cast by an object in a drawing or painting

speech bubble (SPEECH BUH buhl) — in comic strips or comic books, the outlined area (an oval, rectangle, or similar) where words are written to indicate what a character has said

Index

cartoon action 18, 19
cartooning 15, 21
color
  bleed 6, 7
  blending 14
  laying down 8, 10
  overlaying 9, 10
comic books 15, 20
doodling 17
emblem art 27
faces (drawing) 13
lettering 23, 24, 25
permanent ink markers 6, 29
pointillism 9
political cartoon 4
primary colors 8
shading 11
shadowing 11
water-based markers 6, 16

Further Reading

- Bradley, Susannnah, *How to Draw Cartoons*, Henderson Publishing & The Mad Hatter, Inc., 1990.
- Brookes, Mona, *Drawing with Children*, G.P. Putnam's Sons, 1996.
- Cummings, Pat, *Talking with Artists*, Simon & Schuster, 1992.
- Cummings, Pat, *Talking with Artists Vol. II*, Simon & Schuster, 1995.
- Kistler, Mark, *Drawing in 3-D with Mark Kistler*, Simon & Schuster, 1998.
- Kistler, Mark, *Drawing in 3-D Wacky Workbook*, Simon & Schuster, 1998.
- Martin, Judy (editorial consultant), *Painting and Drawing*, Millbrook, 1993.
- Martin, Judy, *Sketching School*, Reader's Digest Association, 1991.
- Murrison, Todd, *Marker Rendering*, Walter Foster Publishing, 1995.
- Thompson, Kimberly Boehler and Loftus, Diana Standing, *Art Connections*, GoodYearBooks, 1995.

SUNDANCE